I looked for HELP. I found it.

on YOU

IT'S OKA to watc other

I can't WAIT to see hat you do next

SUCCEED

you CAN get through this

I Can't WAIT to see what you do

NEVER look back. walk TALL, act fine

hero

you STR

GRIT your TEETH & focus on YOU

you are STRONG

next

You are RESILIENT

keep Smi you

& being yo

never FORGET to TAKE CARE of YOU

Be the person you've always wanted to be

you are MORE than a REFLECTION OF YOU in a mirror

never FORGET to TAKE CARE OF YOU

DON'T l the wor CHANGE

NEVER look back. walk TALL, act fine

Talking about it all IS OKAY, not wanting to IS OKAY too

GRIT your TEETH & focus on YOU

I looked for HELP. I found it.

WE maki & ther LIG

I Can't WAIT to see what you do next

IT

you are my hero

help

keep Smiling & being you. DON'T let the world CHANGE YOU

You are your own NUMBER ONE

you are STRONG you are MORE

YOU must be responsible for your OWN happiness

You are RESILIENT

you CAN get through this

you are excellent TA & you will continue to be so, so DON'T GIVE UP, maybe have a cry and then crack on.

WRITE IT all down

Edited by Hannah Todd
Graphic Design and Cover Design by Jenny Howard
You can find Jenny at www.behance.net/jennywednesday

Published by Hello Me It's You
Hello Me, It's You is a registered charity.
Registered Charity Number: 1171224

First Published October 2016
Second Edition July 2018
Printed by Ingram Spark, United Kingdom.
ISBN 978-0-9935779-2-5

## A COLLECTION OF LETTERS BY YOUNG ADULTS ABOUT THEIR EXPERIENCES WITH MENTAL HEALTH ISSUES

# CONTENTS

## HELLO ME, IT'S YOU

is a charity working towards making
the world a better place for young
adults with mental health issues.
How? Well...

# OUR AIMS AS A CHARITY

**To join the conversation around mental health.**

Recently, mental health has entered the spotlight and some high-profile names are jumping in on the conversation. We would like to add our voices, as young people, to an issue which affects a large number of us.

**To normalise mental health issues and reduce a bit of the negative stigma.**

We hope that by showing that young people of different ages and backgrounds experience mental health problems, we are demonstrating that for a large amount of the population mental health issues are a normality. Our hope is that by revealing it could be you, your sibling, your children or other family members and friends who might be affected by mental health problems, more people are likely to be empathetic and respectful to those already affected.

**To help make young adults who are going through mental health problems, and their families, more comfortable and to stay hopeful.**

## HELLO ME, IT'S YOU

*I don't use the term "teen angst". I prefer the more accurate
"teen unhappiness" or even more accurately, "unhappiness."*

- @Patrick_Ness [10:07am - 19 Sep 2015]

The little book before you is a collection of letters by young
people to their younger selves about their mental health
experiences. It came about when we were both at university and
realised there wasn't much out there about mental health for
young people, *by* young people. We understood the need for
young people to recognise themselves in the voices of others
their age, to get advice that feels relevant and to feel a part of a
community. We needed it ourselves.

We asked people aged 17-24 to anonymously submit letters to their younger selves about their experiences with mental health issues... and they did! We were overwhelmed with the amount of letters we received and the amount of support from well-wishers. As a result we've established the Hello Me, it's You project into a charity. That way we can publish more books and continue to help young people. We do school visits and are always on the look out for more submissions for future books. If you want to find out more or get involved then visit our website at www.hellomeitsyou.org.

We really hope this book helps you. If it does, please do share it with a friend, family member or loved one. One in four people suffer from mental health issues and you never know who you might help by passing this little book on...

Love,
Han & Jen
xx

you are
STRONG

HANNAH

# *You are strong*

I'm 20 now. Weird huh? I'm writing to you because I've just started this big project. I'm making a book about Mental Health. I'm not writing it or anything, don't get too excited. I'm collating loads of letters by people to their 16 year old selves... hence this one to you. When I say this book is about Mental Health, it sounds scary doesn't it? It shouldn't though. A lot of people deal with mental health issues Han, and I hate to break it to you, but you're one of them. And you know what? That's okay. It's not the end of the world. When you're nearly me, you're going to be diagnosed with mild depression and anxiety.

You're going to feel weird about it, it'll make you re-evaluate a whole ton of stuff and you'll change a lot as a result. But I'm not going to drop that bombshell and leave, I've got some hints and tips, okay? So don't worry.

1.    This hopefully won't be too much of a shock and should make some sense. You've already had your first panic attack, you just didn't realise at the time that's what it was. Remember that time you ended up having to sit under a towel crying and hyperventilating while your friend had a shower, as she didn't want to leave you alone? That's what that was! That was a bad one. It was terrifying and you had no idea what was happening (thank you to that friend by the way, she was pretty fab). Then it eased off. You got smaller recurring ones but it got better. You occasionally get some now (for some reason when you pick up the phone at work to make a call but not answer one. They're only mild but certainly not comfortable), but you have help and support from people around you and things are getting better. That will be a recurring theme, things get better.

2.    You are strong. You know that you thrive on helping others. You need to remember that doesn't make you weak when you need to ask for help in return. It also doesn't make the thing which pushes you over the edge silly, if it doesn't measure up in your head to the other things you've faced and been fine with. You still don't have a huge sense of self worth but occasionally

you take yourself by surprise, because you can be great too, and I'm working on it, I promise.

3.     You will learn so much from that experience which contributes towards you going and getting diagnosed. Yes, I could tell you what that experience is and what you've learned but I'm not gonna. Do you know why? Because even though it's horrible and crappy, it's good for you. We both know you probably wouldn't listen anyway right? The point is, I can now look back on that experience and smile, so it can't be too bad right?

4.     You're going to need to protect your sister. You won't understand, but the fact you try will probably help. I'm only starting to understand now and that's as a result of my own experiences with mental health wobbles. That's another bonus of this mental health thing, you learn how to relate to others. She will get there and she's doing fab now, but just be there to stand next to her when she needs it.

5.     Words are still your escape. You'll come to love poetry (performance poetry, not the stuff you weren't all that excited about at GCSE). You still read lots and now you've got a job where you get to help authors find their way to publication… and you get paid for that! Speaking of which…

6.    You have a part time job that you really, truly love. You have an amazing group of friends and the same fantastic family. Hopefully, we will finish Uni having done alright too. You've been to the other side of the world (TREASURE THAT! It's still been the best experience I've had yet) and lots of places in between. You've met one of your heroes, sung until your voice goes, laughed until your belly has ached and cried a bit too. You've made yourself proud and embarrassed and sad and angry and happy and it's been fab.

I'm not going to pretend sometimes I don't struggle but I'm staying pretty positive about it all. You have so much fun ahead of you, I'm getting excited just think about it. And you know what's even cooler? I've got even more ahead of me.

Han x

Talking about it all IS OKAY, not wanting to IS OKAY too

# *Talking about it all is okay, not wanting to talk about it is okay too*

It's okay to be alone, sometimes being alone helps you work it out, at your own pace, with your own thoughts, in your own safe space... that's definitely long walks around and around and about, preferably somewhere with some greenness involved. Take your camera, maybe focus on getting a good a close up of a bumble bee.

You don't need to feel alone, or lonely, though. There is always someone there, at the end of the phone, down the road, a short way away, you know people close to you, or even people that aren't, who will listen to you or hug you or talk it out... without judgement. Talking about it all is okay, not wanting to talk about it is okay too, don't feel guilty either way!

Writing helps, but try not to dwell on the sad things you've recorded. Try to treat it as a deep breath, pushing away and writing out what's going on inside, then try to close the notebook and watch something funny. The funniest will probably be the Bridesmaid's aeroplane scene. That will come out soon – or 'You've Been Framed'. Eventually you will reach a point where you can write some positive things alongside the negative.

The sadness never goes. You won't ever forget him. The time will help you deal with it all, and the people you meet along the way make your life fulfilled, you will laugh more, and dwell less.

Oh and remember to swim or jog or kickbox......

Anonymous, 23 years old

you are
MORE
than a
"REFLECTION
in a mirror

# *You are more than a reflection in a mirror*

Hello me, it's you… 8 years from now! Pretty crazy, isn't it?! Today I've decided to write to you – yes you, little pretty thing – to give you a glimpse into the future. I feel like I have so much to tell you… You wouldn't believe everything that has happened within the last few years. Yes, for a start, you're living in the UK and you're actually speaking English! Didn't see that coming, did you?

Well there is a lot you probably haven't seen coming. You're only at the beginning of an amazing journey and it has been full of highs, and I'm afraid some lows as well…

But fear not, it is all going to be O K A Y.

By now, you've probably realised that your relationship with food is a never ending love/hate relationship. Food is as much your best friend as your worse enemy. You like spending hours in the kitchen but as little time as possible in front of a plate. For the moment you think there's nothing unusual to that, despite your friends starting to get worried about your tiny legs... And you're right, it's not unusual, but it doesn't make it less important. It is really essential that you are aware of this and that you accept it as a condition.

In 2015, you will finally see a specialist to get help to overcome your bulimia. I know, that sounds scary and ugly, but trust me, this is the best thing which can happen to you. You're probably thinking that it can't be right, because eating disorders only happen to others and that you are strong enough to deal with your problems by yourself. Well no, eating disorders can happen to anyone and they are really common. They vary in degrees and forms, and have different origins. They can affect anyone and it is crucial that you remember this, so that, when the day comes, you don't feel guilty about the way you feel or act because guilt will be your biggest enemy. And until you don't feel guilty about being you, simply you, you will not feel better.

So here is some advice to help you get through the next few years:

Get out of your shell and talk to people. As soon as you open up to your loved ones, the solitude and loneliness will lessen. Your best friend – who you haven't met yet but is the most wonderful person in the whole universe – and your mum – who will send you the greatest email back to your "coming out" – will be special allies;

Accept that you need help. There is nothing wrong about getting help and your problem is as important as anyone else's problem. I know that you are always the one helping people, but sometimes, it is important that you accept being helped too;

Realise that your body is your best friend – cherish it, love it, nurture it! You need to work with your body, not against it;

Your appearance is not a reflection of your Self. You are more than a reflection in a mirror;

There is no such thing as perfection. Stop striving for the impossible and just be yourself;

You are not weird. Other people have the same problem and act like you. Even though your comportment isn't a healthy behaviour, it is common and treatable. Accept it and talk about it freely. It is not shameful to have bulimia;

You are worth being loved;

Everything is as it should be and you are responsible for your own happiness. Stop waiting for external things to make your life better. Learn to live with what you have and cherish every little thing.

All of this may sound cheesy at the moment and I get that. But if you accept it, trust me, you will have won half of the battle. Life is a funny thing, and you will learn more about yourself and the world every day. In a few years, you are going to discover the most amazing thing that is, Yoga. At first, you will go as a means to stretch. And then, you will find that it is a lot more than this and you will get into the spiritual side of it a lot. And eventually, you'll get a qualification to be an instructor. Doesn't it sound amazing?

So, yeah, I don't have solutions to all our problems, and I probably never will. But it is okay because life is about learning from our experiences and living in the present moment. Everything is O K A Y.

Love, L

Anonymous, 24 years old

never
FORGET to
TAKE CARE
OF YOU

ANONYMOUS, 24

# *Never forget to take care of you*

Hello me, it's you.

I'm writing to you because the idea for this book really spoke to me and could have helped me over the last 8 years, so will hopefully help other young people going through similar issues. So right now you're still living in Wales, you're getting ready for your GCSEs and you have good relationships with your step family (well done by the way, they're a tricky family). You have already been through some tough times, but... now don't freak out... things are going to get a little worse. Not horrendous by any means. Everyone you love is safe and well, so if we keep things in perspective things are never that bad, but it will feel pretty bad at the time.

You are about to move across the country leaving behind dad, your friends, the boy you love and you're going to attend a college where you know nobody. At the moment you are scared, and that is okay because it's a big deal; most people your age stay in their school for sixth form or go to a college that most of their friends will be attending too. But remain calm, because people are actually quite nice and there is no need to be so scared of them. All those thoughts you have of "they think I'm stupid" or "they don't want to talk to me" or all of that, that is a very common negative thinking pattern called mind reading, and believe it or not, you can't read minds. You have no idea what people are thinking when you speak to them and you can't predict how they will react either. You are a smart, interesting and funny person – over the last few years we have been described as the life of the party! – so people actually want to talk to you and hear what you have to say. Don't be afraid to say something, or even nothing. People like to talk so listening is a good way to make friends too. Also, it is not your responsibility to direct 100% of a conversation, so never feel pressured to fill all the silences. Silences in conversation are normal. If you're in a group of 5 people, you only need to fill 20% of the conversation, which is hardly any, so relax.

The move to England will create some other problems too, and things will get pretty dark for a while, but you do the right thing and seek help and you will be in counselling for sixth months of college. Your counsellor is wonderful. She makes you smile, looks out for you when things get really tough, and actually sets you on the path to following psychology. Over the next few years you will spend another year in counselling during your time at university and beyond. There is nothing wrong with that, and more importantly there is nothing wrong with you. There is only so much crap one person can deal with by themselves, and you happen to deal with a lot. Because you are a good friend, sister and daughter, lots of people turn to you for help with their own problems. Remember that you're allowed to ask for some space from this, as always being relied upon for advice and secrecy is exhausting and mentally draining. Never forget to take care of you.

At one point, Mum will move to France, and you will convince yourself that she doesn't love you, which probably stems from your fear of abandonment. Didn't know you had that did you? Remember those dreams as a kid of dad disappearing? Well that's the effect that mum and dad's divorce had. Don't worry, she loves you and misses you, and will be very happy when she moves back. When they are teenagers, your sisters will need you. They will both disclose to you something very separate but very serious while they are living in France. Try not to panic, or do anything rash. There is nothing you can really do other than be there for them to talk to when they need to, and be a shoulder to cry on. I know they've never been very good at reciprocating in your relationship with them, and they're still no good at it now, but you will be there for them regardless because you're a good person.

Sexuality plagues you for a few years, so here is some reassurance. You are straight, and when you are in your twenties you will meet the most wonderful man who you love more than you ever thought you could and he feels the same about you. Therefore, if you want to experiment, there is nothing wrong with that. It actually helps to find who you are and what you want out of life. Don't be so scared about it.

Speaking of the boyfriend, trust him. He is it, everything. He will fall in love with you by the end of your first date, so don't fret any time he doesn't reply to a text straight away or spends time with his brother and not you. The anxiety in this relationship also stems from your fear of abandonment, but he will not leave you. Ever. Despite the struggles over the last 8 years, now: I have a 2:1 degree in Psychology; was a member of two society committees during university; learned how to publicly speak, to the extent of co-presenting a whole evening to 300 people including CEOs and MPs; have a couple of groups of friends who genuinely love me; own my own business, which I love; and I live in my own flat. You are so much stronger than you think. Writing this letter to you has only just made me realise how strong we are. There are difficult things to come, but try not to dwell on them because for every difficult time there are so many wonderful times that every moment is worth it, I promise.

Anonymous, 24 years old

WE'RE
making it
3 there is
LIGHT

ANONYMOUS, 21

# *We're making it and there is light*

Hello me, it's you.

So I'm turning 21 soon and you know what? Life's going really well! Being 16 was tough, I'm not going to lie to you it was probably one of the hardest years of our life to date, but I have news for you. We made it! We got to university, not only that, we've just started third year! I won't lie to you, what's gone on inbetween then and now hasn't been easy but we still made it! So here's what's happened in our lives:

CBT didn't work... I can hear you saying "again?!"but the fact is we didn't really want to do it, so why should it work? You know what, it doesn't matter. We've learned our own coping strategies and believe it or not we have shoulder length hair (well, everywhere but the top)! R's getting married this summer and she wants me in a tiara so I'm really trying. This year's been tough, mums been through hell and back at work and so to have any hair left is a miracle on its own.

You got us that Maths GCSE and the atmosphere in Jersey was amazing! Thanks to you we're where we are now. I won't lie to you A levels were hard. Harder than we ever thought they would be. Psychology was tough but you stuck at it and with the help of the staff we made it out with a pass. Mum and Dad really do regret not letting us go sooner, yes the bus and walk is long but its worth it because we're happy there.

Moving to university was tough. We got homesick in the first few weeks but we didn't break, we didn't go home and you met one of the most amazing friends ever and guess what?! She knows everything: the anxiety, the trichotillomania and the depression. I was terrified she'd think I was a freak and never speak to me again but she didn't. She's still the only one outside of family who knows about that side of us but her reaction made me wonder if I'd made it into more of a skeleton in the closet than it needed to be, guess we'll never know.

I guess what I want you to know is it gets better, you haven't had a visible patch since year 11 and we haven't been anywhere near as down as we were in past. Life is still hard and it's an ongoing battle but we're making it and there is light; this time next year I'll have graduated with QTS and that's something I wasn't sure would ever happen. Dad's still dad, mum's still mum, but we've made it to 21 and we'll make it the rest of the way too.

Love, Me.

                                        Anonymous, 21 years old

you are not
worthless
and you can
ASK FOR
help

ANONYMOUS, 20

# *You are not worthless and you can ask for help*

Hello me, It's you.

I'm 20 now and not that long ago I got diagnosed with borderline personality disorder. Don't worry, I know it's scary at first but once you know what it means you learn to understand it. I know you've been going through a lot at the moment but remember you've got people who do care about you no matter how much you don't think they do. Remember all those times you cut yourself? Don't feel so guilty, you are not alone in this, there are so many people out there that are suffering in silence just like you!

I know you are with that guy at the moment and not too far away it's going to hurt, but remember to breathe and that someone will love you again; you are not as worthless as you think you are. I know you don't know who you are right now or what you're going to do with yourself, I still feel that way now, but it gets easier. You'll learn to think about the present and being aware of everything around you, it's a great feeling and I'm still learning other skills too.

Remember all those times we hurt people and said nasty things? Go apologise, tell them you didn't mean it and that you were overwhelmed. Tell them that they mean something to you, tell them that one day it will make sense to them too. I remember all those times we felt so overwhelmed by our emotions just by the simplest things, it's like everything is heightened, like we don't have a rational mind, like every little thing is exaggerated, you over analyse everything even things as simple as your friend not being able to meet you. You're paranoid that you're going to lose people, so you do everything in your power to not do that, even doing stuff that could harm you or ruin relationships.

You know those times we thought we heard people talking even though when you went to check they weren't there and we were so frightened, well that still happens sometimes, more so when we are stressed but don't worry it's not as scary any more because we understand why now. I know sometimes you're going to want to give up and at some points your even going to try it but remember you are loved, you are not worthless and you can ask for help. Things will get better, you will start making a go of things and I'm still learning now and I'm going to carry on learning new skills on how to cope, I'm going to keep spreading awareness and do you want to know why?

Because we are not alone.

Anonymous, 20 years old

You are
¿ excellent
? you will continue
to be so, so DON'T
GIVE UP, maybe have
a cry and then
Crack on.

*You are excellent and you will continue to be so, so don't give up, maybe have a cry and then crack on*

Hello me, it's you.

I hope you've had a good day. And I hope you are feeling happy because I know that sometimes things are scary. Everything will be absolutely fine. I promise. Your anxiety is something that will not disappear, so you need to learn to deal with it sooner rather than later. You have probably already had your first panic attack and no one really took it seriously. And that's okay but you need to know that you can help yourself.

You can find people to talk to, the counsellor at school or the doctor. Anxiety is horrible and it feels shameful and embarrassing. Take a deep breath and do it, just like you did when you were thirteen and arranged to see the counsellor. (Also if you could start dealing with it now it would make life easier for me at 21!) There is nothing wrong with you. You are NOT mad. I promise.

Over the next few years you're going to go through some difficult times – you might feel useless and broken and unworthy. Please try not to feel like this. Trust in your decisions and follow what makes you happy. If you are not happy somewhere then get out.

When you feel mad or bad or empty, write about it (I know, feelings, mehhh), or draw or talk to your friends. Try not to turn to food. Because that escalates. And you have far too much to offer the world to spend your time preoccupied with food, counting calories, sneaking biscuits and surviving on satsumas. So just don't even start. Please. You are beautiful and worthy and exactly how you are meant to be.

You are going to make an amazing friend after the summer and she will show you exactly what a best friend should be. Help her and she will help you. (And try not to be too mean to her boyfriend, you will never think anyone is good enough for her). And when you are at the right university you will make the best friends ever and you will wonder how you ever lived without these people and you will tell them everything. And you will help them. Because you are all a bit weird together which is good. You already have anxiety and OCD (go and see a doctor now and they will tell you this, better when you're 16 than when you're 22), but unfortunately when you are about 20 you will start to pull out your eyebrows. You wont be able to stop. So go and see a doctor. It sucks, but it has a somewhat entertaining name – trichotillomania.

If the doctor doesn't help, go and see another one, and another one until they help. Because they really will, but sometimes you have to find the right one. Know that where you are right now is where you are meant to be and that everything will be okay. The next few years will be amazing and when they're tough you will learn from them.

You are excellent and you will continue to be so, so don't give up, maybe have a cry and then crack on. And see a damn doctor. Now.

So that's my advice. Good luck, be brave and don't worry too much, it's just life.

Anonymous, 22 years old

I would like you to know that THERE IS SOMEBODY out there who loves you

ANONYMOUS, 19

# *I would like you to know that there is somebody out there who loves you*

I was around the age of 12 or 13 when it started to feel like it was raining everyday and that there was no spot of sunlight or rainbows in my world, only dark, black clouds that followed me everywhere, that didn't seem to fade. I started looking around at other people at school, trying to figure out what 'normal' meant. Did they cry all the time? Did other people think about hurting themselves on a regular basis? That was just a typical teenage thing, right? I would grow out of it eventually, wouldn't I? Obviously I didn't ask anyone these questions, the thought of telling people how I thought and felt was just too much to bear. I was scared that they would misunderstand.

So, I decided to put on a shield of armour and act all tough and brave and that I would have to hide it - "fake it till you make it" I told myself. But, that didn't exactly go to plan. I ended up becoming a very angry, destructive, rude person, who took everything out on anyone. I pushed away the people who cared about me the most. I was just so maddened at the world for feeling the way I did, that I blamed my sadness on others. I now realise it was probably because I was too scared to admit I wasn't okay. I didn't want anyone thinking I was 'weak'.

Instead, of growing out of it, I fell much, much deeper into the never ending tunnel of darkness, I couldn't seem to shake off all the anger, sadness and hurt that was inside of me. It began to get to the point where I saw death as my only option. Everything hurt so much - everything required backbreaking strength. The thought of having to face another day killed me. It hurt so much just to simply exist that I became very, very close to wiping out the light and evaporate into darkness.

At some of the pitch-black darkest times of my life, the thought of not existing and having no thoughts and feelings was so peaceful. I felt irreparably broken, that there was nothing anything or anyone could do to help me, BUT, something stopped me - a tiny spark of audacity that I had to dig very deep inside of me to find and fight incredibly hard to cling to. For a while 99.9% of me wanted to cease to exist, but there was that tiny 00.1% that kept on flickering alight inside of me, though it was hardly visible on a daily basis, I decided to find some kind of faith, if it was even there at all. The point is, when your mind turns on you, it's extremely hard to fight it, but you don't have to battle it all together at once. Fighting it is an intensifying process, and yet all it takes is the smallest effort such as waking up and saying "No, not today" to send your demons the message that you will not be their victim.

These small achievements have added up, and here I am, still here, several years later. Yeah, these past few years have been the toughest of them all, but those were the years I am so glad to have lived, I have met some wonderful people, people who were worth waiting and living for and I have had some amazing experiences. Obviously, you don't get from "I want to die." to "I'm so happy I am still here" in one step. Everyone's steps are different, it can take weeks, months or even years, it doesn't matter, what only matters is that you hold on, regardless of how long and what path you take to recovery, I know that you are capable of making it and that recovery is possible.

If you are feeling like I was I few years ago and are considering suicide, I have a few words to say to you: I would like you to know that there is somebody out there who loves you, some of you won't believe me, and some of you know that there are, but you aren't sure it's enough. You can't feel, see or believe it because you simply don't understand how anyone could see anything about you worth loving and that everything seems so dark and sad and there is that one thought that you cannot seem to get rid of " Maybe everyone is better off without me." I know, believe me, I know. What you are feeling is sadness beyond sadness and it's so incredibly hard to picture any way to escape it. People who have never felt this way do not understand it, they will tell you to "get over it" or that you are "just being a teenager" or that "everyone gets sad sometimes" those people aren't trying to be hurtful, they just don't have the knowledge or experience that other people's brains don't work like theirs do.

But honestly, trust me, there are many, many people out there who know how you feel, who understand, who will not judge, or dismiss your pain, including me, but you have to ask for help. You have to be willing to let someone in. Do tell someone, even if it is something as simple as "I don't feel good, and I think I need some help" it's a huge step. Please do not hold these horrible thoughts inside. I speak from experience – and they don't go away on their own, but with a little help and time, they DO eventually go away. You can open up to anyone you trust, a friend, a counsellor, a relative, etc. If you don't have anyone in your life you feel comfortable talking to, call a suicide hotline, a crisis centre, or a hospital, especially if you are actively suicidal. This is why I am telling you, that as someone who has been thrown off a precipice into the deepest, darkest pit: that you are not alone, you are not worthless, and that you are SO much stronger that you think you are, even if you just managed to open your eyes and breathe today, then you - yes, YOU, are so, so brave and tough.

I'm not sure how I can tell you exactly how to find that little spark of light inside of you, but what I do know, is that because you are here right now and reading this, that that little light of yours is there, somewhere. It can get better, you will get better and all of the things that seem so painful now, will eventually lift and life will seem worth living again. You are worth something, you are worth saving, your life matters. Maybe you can't see that now, but you will. Because you can get better. You will. I promise. One day you will get up in the morning and laugh and think, "I'm still here motherfuckers" and run down the stairs into another day.

Someone out there loves you.

Anonymous, 19 years old

keep Smiling

3. being you.

DON'T let

the world

CHANGE you

ANONYMOUS, 22

# *Keep smiling and being you. Don't let the world change you.*

Dear 16 year old me,

You will be 22 in 6 years time. Right now you will feel as if you are on top of the world and that nothing can touch you. Do not worry, you will come out with 2A*'s, 5A's and 2 B's in your GCSEs. You will be named hockey captain, so don't stop training. Keep smiling and being you. Don't let the world change you. Don't let school work stress you out. Do not choose to do the International Baccalaureate. Go back and carry on with your A Levels. It will be the best decision you will ever make. Let me tell you why:

Stress, anxiety and depression will become the benefactors of our lives. It will be a constant non-stop roller coaster of ups and downs. In your final year of IB, do not stress. Please, I beg of you, do not stress yourself out. Otherwise we end up where we are now. Memory-less. How you ask? Stress. Epilepsy will become the norm, and having to live with amnesia after that will make life even more difficult. We will become a victim to bullying for 3 years after. Be strong. Don't be weak. Don't show them your weakness. Smile. Laugh. Enjoy life. Right now, we are showing the world that being a 'cabbage' was a thing of the past. We are successful. Remember that.

Don't let depression get the better of you. Keep working out. You will become infertile if you don't because of the weight gain. It is tough to deal with PCOS and finish university with no memory. Be happy. Don't stop smiling. I know, it is tough sometimes. Mom and Dad still won't understand and will have major expectations. Keep smiling. Love yourself. Stop straightening your hair so much. Embrace your curls. PCOS will get the better of our hair by 22 and we will end up bald. Please. Don't cut our beautiful hair.

During the break between IB and University, please get our leg operation done. Don't be afraid of that pain. By 22 your spine will have twisted and will make walking, running and climbing steps painful. We will not have any time after this.

Planning a future is difficult, one that will accommodate all of our sicknesses. No one will understand your daily pain. Keep smiling. Don't let depression from the pain darken your day. Life is stunning, beautiful, amazing.

Keep smiling. Laughing. Loving life. Don't stop what we love doing. Go the extra mile. Don't let people rule your life or bring you down. Find a job to get out the house and away from the fights. You will be happier. Get away from the tension, maybe then we won't lose our memory. As I sit here and write you this letter, my dear 16 year old self, I find much sadness at how much you will have endure in these coming years. At 22 you will feel 60. Don't let life suck the happiness out. Keep smiling. Laughing. Don't be afraid to date that boy. You would rather love than have not loved at all. Don't be so shy. Laugh. Smile. Giggle. You will eventually get over depression, but anxiety will take over. We are still working to get through this, but I promise you: WE WILL BE FINE.

Love yourself. No one else will love you as much as yourself.

Love from,

J

As much as you SAY that you CANNOT & will not— I promise you, YOU CAN & YOU will

*As much as you say that you cannot and will not - I promise you, you can and you will*

Hello Me at 16 years old, it's you (just four years down the line),

Mental Health has always played a big part of your life. I say played, but really, there's been no competition involved – a lot of the time, it has won every single game. As I look back, I realise that you have had parts of it carved into your soul since you were a toddler. Mum and Dad have always referred to you as a worrier, but in the next few years, you'll terrify them to the point where they too become the ones that are worrying.

I know that OCD, Trichotillomania, Self Harm and Depression are already four weights that are tying you down, often making life seem like an impossible chore; a chore that you're finding it increasingly hard to accomplish. I also know that you're trying to hold on really tight, with everything that you have, but I need you to do me a favour, and hold on a little tighter, for a little while longer. It feels unbearable; worse than anybody could ever imagine, but you need to find a way to keep your grip. As much as you say that you cannot and will not - I promise you, you can and you will (otherwise I would not be here writing you this letter).

The reason that I say this is because as much as it pains me to tell you; during the next couple of years, it's going to get even harder. You are going to scream, cry, and curse at the world for being so painfully unfair. You are going to spend some days wishing you were dead, and countless nights terrified that you're going to die. It will not make sense. Depression will exhaust you of everything that you have, and Anxiety is going to strip you bare of everything that you are.

Above and beyond all, it is going to hurt like hell. There will be numerous doctors and therapists, who you know do not understand, and for that reason, you begin to form a strong dislike towards them all. It will all come to a head when you're admitted to hospital twice, seven months apart. You will be away from home for months, and at the time, you stupidly see this as a good thing. There will be long days and lonely nights, patients who become your hospital family, and tears shed in the bucket load.

You will see things that no teenager or young adult should ever have to, and it will make you question everything, even more than you already did. You will get sick of people, and you will become beyond tired of yourself. You will soon realise that a lot of the people in your life simply cannot comprehend you or your mental health, and for this reason, they will get up and leave – each one of them leaving a scar on your already-hurting heart. By the time you are my age, you will have gained many scars; both physically and emotionally, and as much as you'll probably be judged for them, all you were doing was trying to survive.

That is one of the most important things that I need you to hold on to – You will survive. When the noise of life becomes too much and you feel more alone than you ever deemed possible – you will survive. When people leave and the days hurt – you are going to survive. When things are hard at home and Dad is too sick to bear, you and he will both survive. When the anxiety is making you shake with fear and you don't think you're going to live until the sun arises tomorrow – you will survive that, too.
I am writing you this as if I now have every aspect of my life

put together, but that's not entirely the case. On the bad days, I still often wish that I had somebody telling me the things that I am now telling you, but I guess it's easier for me to do this, because I know you well. You'll soon find out that every day is always going to be a struggle and all these years later, I still hurt like you do now. Distraction is key - it always has been. Our mental health is always going to dwindle – There will be days, months, and weeks where you're in control, then all it will take is one argument, one bad day, one trigger to make you wonder if anything in life is worth it. It is though; it's worth it every time. It's always going to be one step forward, closely followed by two thousand steps back, but one day, we'll find a way to make it. We will.

I want you to know, with everything that I am, that we are, that one day it's going to be time for us to leave this sadness behind. You'll begin to cling to it, as I am now; metaphorical blisters on both your hands and soul, because you're too afraid to let go of a life that you're now so used to. When it's time, we are going to have to let it go.

One day, when you're just 17, and sitting on the floor in tears after a bad day, somebody important will say to you "If you had a broken leg, people could see that you were hurting and you could get help. You haven't got a broken leg, but you're in so much pain, and you need help, you need to get it sorted". That,

I believe, is the most important thing about mental health – It hurts just as much as any broken limb or open wound; the only difference is that you cannot physically see it in it's entirety.

One day, my friend, we will get it sorted.

From,
You at 20 years of age.

Anonymous, 20 years old

No MATTER what love ♥ throws at you, you have to BELIEVE in it.

ANONYMOUS, 20

## *No matter what love throws at you, you have to believe in it.*

Fearless is falling madly in love again, even though you've been hurt before. Fearless is walking into your freshman year of high school at fifteen. Fearless is getting back up and fighting for what you want over and over again - even though every time you've tried before, you've lost.

To me, "fearless" is not the absence of fear.
It's not being completely unafraid.
To me, fearless is having fears.
Fearless is having doubts.
Lots of them.

To me, fearless is living in spite of those things that scare you to death.

I think loving someone despite what people think is fearless. I think allowing yourself to cry on the bathroom floor is fearless. Letting go is fearless. Then, moving on and being alright - that's fearless too.

But no matter what love throws at you, you have to believe in it. You have to believe in love stories and Prince Charmings and happily ever after.

Anonymous, 20 years old

"Stay TRUE
STAY
STRONG
Stay happy"

ANONYMOUS, 20

# *Stay true, stay strong, stay happy*

Hello me, it's you

This letter is not designed to bring you down, or scare you, or make you rethink your choices; this will be cathartic (for 20 year old me anyway).

Just around the corner is a difficult and dark period in your life, unfortunately there is nothing you can do about it so the best option would've been to face it head on, however you being you, you went and decided to not do that. Not talking about it to someone was a bad idea. What I'm telling you is that very soon you will realise that you are slipping into depression and it will last longer than any previous bad spell. It will come about due to numerous factors, however I'm fairly certain that it began with N.

N is beautiful, and although I haven't seen her since I was 18, I'm sure she's still out there somewhere, being beautiful. The way her hair swung across her eyes, her infectious laugh and the way she puts her tongue between her teeth when she smiles will never be forgotten. You love her because she's a good person and you can see no flaw in her. However this love for her will (in my opinion) began to send you into a depressive state. Your overthinking and overactive brain (which unfortunately still hasn't gone away) will have you analysing every possible reason why she doesn't love you back, why you aren't together and will you ever be together. Your dreams at night will not do you any favours either. Next will come exams that you didn't care about or even think you should be taking. They feel like they will never end and you will feel that you are not smart enough (which you are, you're just crap at exams!).

These factors will weigh on your mind, for what feels like an eternity. However some things will bring you joy, seeing your friends, sitting in the sunshine and listening to music (especially music, never stop listening to music!). Hold on to the things that bring you joy, because I'm glad to say that even though I am not completely happy yet, it will take time, but things do get better. Now you have a job where you can work outside in the sunshine so you can go travelling, you have discovered more amazing music than you could possibly imagine and you still hang out with your friends and have a good time. And although you can't see the light at the end of the tunnel, I'm sure that for both of us there are only a few more corners to round.

So I'll leave you with this, the three things that I learnt from being depressed, and I know that you'll live your life by them:

- Treat others as you wish to be treated
- All knowledge is good knowledge
- See the beauty in everything

Stay true, stay strong, stay happy and keep listening to music, you know it makes sense.

From
Anon

Anonymous, 20 years old

WRITE IT
all down
& TRUST ME
It will help

# *Write it all down and trust me it will help*

Hello me, it's you,

You've written this letter in your head a thousand and one times, and you've tried to work out the best way to warn yourself of what's yet to come. You're 16, and things aren't going great now are they? I'm sorry to tell you, it gets worse before it gets better. But it does get better, and you faced the worst and you're a hell of a lot stronger now because of it. This all sounds quite intense, it's not supposed to. Let me explain.

Firstly, let me start by saying that just because you feel the way you do, that does not make you different, strange, or inadequate in any way. It is a blessing and a curse to feel things so deeply, so own it at the best of times and ride it out in the darker times. You are not just hormonal or overreacting. You are depressed and unwell. Say it out loud, it's okay, you can't pretend it isn't real forever. Just breathe. You can do this. You do not have to cope with this by yourself so please don't shut yourself away from everyone who loves you. They want to help you, sometimes they just don't know how.

Write it down. How you're feeling I mean. Write it all down and trust me it will help. Keep breathing. Ride out the panic. It's overwhelming I know, but it will be over soon. Inhale. Exhale. Count to 10. Better? Now things will seem a little darker for a while, and your whole world will turn upside down soon. You will lose some loved ones, and a lot of things will break apart in front of you. However, I have 3 words to say to you. "You are strong". But my god, you are stubborn (FYI you still are). You don't have to pretend that everything is fine, when you look back at this time, you'll realise just how not fine it actually all was. You are feeling so lost, and so broken and as if you have nothing left to give or to hold onto. I can tell you now, that is not true. This will be the making of you, and you will turn your life around. Your support network is fantastic and you have people in your life who would be by your side picking you up in an instant. You get a great job and meet some great people, you get some awesome experience and then (bombshell), you go to uni! You help others, you support them and you love them. You find something you are so passionate about, so stop worrying that you'll never fit in or amount to anything, because it is just not true.

So, in the next 4 years, you're going to meet some people who will change your life, who have all moulded you in some way or another. Some of these people will hurt you, but most will still be in your life now, and you should really thank them for just sticking around even when you tried with everything you had to push them away. Your family is a little different nowadays, but still just as amazing as always. And your best friends save your life on a daily basis.

So even though there are bad days, you have so many adventures awaiting you. Bad days still come around, but you know yourself well enough to cope now. So please stop telling yourself there's nothing left to live for, you have no idea what is around the corner. You are made of tough stuff. You are loved. You are living. You are enough.

Love , (Future you, still as cool as ever)
P.S Vodka is not your friend. It never will be.

Anonymous, 20 years old

you
CAN
get
through
this

ANONYMOUS, 20

# *You can get through it*

Hey there, 16 year old me...

It feels strange to be writing this letter. I just want you to know, despite some of the bad things that happen along the way there's a happy end... or not the end really, a happy new beginning?

I guess you could probably guess by now that you will have some sort of mental health problem, having siblings, parents and grandparents that suffer from severe clinical depression. But I guess you won't have realised that the problem is anxiety. It's that awful feeling of foreboding, that something bad is going to happen at any moment that hangs around you like a dark cloud. The feeling that things will suddenly take a turn for a worst, that you get before a new experience or just a day that you're feeling nervous.

I know your anxiety expresses itself as obsessive skin picking (don't worry, mum will take you to the doctors for that) and that you haven't had your first panic attack yet, but I'm so sorry to tell you they'll be triggered by an abusive relationship and being raped. Those experiences will lead to borderline anorexia and bouts of serious panic attacks- but you can get through it.

Firstly please tell someone! Therapy works wonders! It will help you to come to terms with what has happened, be able to eat again and help keep the panic attacks under control.

I'll never be able to thank enough that friend that was there for me, he'll sit and be with you when you feel like there's no one there, you can trust him and he'll stick by you.

You'll get through this. When you start to feel like the world has been swept from underneath you and you can't breathe, find a quiet place and focus on what's around you. Feel the floor, concentrate on your hands, anything to help you centre yourself. It's alright to take yourself home from the party, there's nothing wrong with watching some films rather than going out if you don't feel up to it, and even something as simple as a colouring book can help calm your mind.

But don't shut yourself away, don't hide yourself! I know some days it will be hard to leave your room but you're a confident person and people will be happy to see you- no matter what your anxiety tells you. You'll have so many great opportunities and experiences in the next few years that you'll be so glad you got out of bed for.

I know it's a lot to take in, but now you're 20, and it's all ok. Your friends and family are all there for you, you've figured out what's important to you and you're willing to go out and get it. You're proud of who you are and looking forward to the journey ahead. And most importantly, that anxiety? It's not a big deal, you can totally handle it.

So here is to the new beginning!
Stay safe, Love you lots x

Anonymous, 20 years old

Be the
person
you've always
wanted
to be

# *Help is out there but it takes a brave soul to go and find it.*

Dear 16 year old me,

I don't really know where to start. The next few years of your life are going to be the happiest and hardest days you have ever experienced... but it'll all be worth it in the end. If I have one piece of advice for you it's "keep going". College is going to transform you, you'll become a confident, popular girl with the world at your feet. Embrace it. Be the person you've always wanted to be. Dye your hair and rip your clothes and stay out all night. Just don't lose who you are. Make sure you do the subjects you WANT to do, don't apply for things you feel you should. Do what it takes to be happy. Don't let people bring you down.

University is going to be tougher. The toughest. I won't sugar coat this because I'm no liar. You're going to feel alone and broken with nowhere to turn. You'll feel trapped and frustrated. But when you're at your lowest you'll seek help. Counselling will make you realise that you're not just feeling like everyone else. You do have a problem that isn't your fault and you need help. Severe Depression is not something to be taken lightly and no one has to do it on their own. You'll cry and cry some more but you'll get medicine. It'll help. It won't be enough but it'll be a start. You'll have your dose doubled and that'll make more of an impact on stopping you from falling too low. There shouldn't be a stigma about taking medication for a mental illness. It's not your fault your brain isn't allowing you to be happy and don't let anyone make you think it is.

Okay so here's the tough bit. First year was hard but second year will be harder (sorry). The people you thought were your friends will destroy the fragile world you kind-of-made. But, funny as this sounds, it'll be the best thing that has ever happened to you. No, honestly! You'll realise that you had changed to try and keep people happy and you lost yourself. Remember that girl at college? You need to find her again and be carefree and confident. Over the year you realised someone negatively affected you way more than you ever realised and you're a shadow of your former self. BUT here's the great thing. You'll find true and beautiful friends in the midst of the pain. You'll be brave enough to let the broken you disappear and break away from the prison you'd been in. You'll be happy again, it'll take time, sure. But the friends you find will make it easy for you and show you how to move on. Never be around people who judge you or make you feel guilty. GO AND BE FREE AND HAPPY.

And you know what? You need to go through the darkest corridors before you really appreciate how great the light and open air really feels. And you know something else? You're the strongest person I know and the most capable girl. You will come through all this stronger than ever. Sure, there'll have been some cuts along the way, some dark circles under your eyes and a fair few tears but in time you'll be able to look down from the mountain you climbed and see how far you've come.

Mental health issues are serious and people should appreciate that. It's tough on kids that don't even know to get help because they think they're making up their troubles. I can talk from experience. Help is out there but it takes a brave soul to go and find it. So a note to anyone going through the same pain... whether you have or haven't got help, just talk to someone about this stuff. Someone you trust. Maybe even someone you don't know, a counsellor or doctor....or even yourself. Write a letter to the current you and let it all out. Bottling up your suffering is the hardest part but the bravest is letting it out. And even if you don't realise it yet, you are brave enough.

Dear 16 year old me. Hi. You're doing great and there are a lot of people who love you. I love you. Most of all realise that I LOVE YOU.

From
You.

P.S. keep going, you're not out of the water yet but keep plodding along and one day you'll be medication free and as happy as Larry.

P.P.S. try and find Larry and see what his trick is for always being so goddamn happy.

Anonymous, 21 years old

"NOBODY can change how YOU feel inside but YOURSELF"

# *Nobody can change how you feel inside but yourself*

The Struggle

It's something I live with everyday,
A constant struggle of binge or starve,
A feeling of emptiness emotionally and physically,
Physically it feels like I am not the way I should look for society,
for clothing stores or for myself,
People say I'm beautiful the way I am, but deep inside, and
through the mirror it's a distorted image.
Is it a binge and purge day? Is it a try to limit myself day?
A constant struggle.

Fad dieting, fasting, my whole life,
Being told I need to lose weight to fit into something, being told
I am too fat from a very young age sticks with you through life,
I would not wish this illness for anybody, it's not just Bulimia,
it's a curse to me, probably for the rest of my life, but I can and
will do my best to fight it.

Since I was 18 I believe it became more apparent,
The curse and illness started, worsened then took over my life,
It was denial then acceptance then help from one person very
close to my heart.

Nobody can change how you feel inside but yourself, this is rule
number one I guess,
It takes a great amount of time,
I am still trying and battling every single day, a simple question
from a friend like "Do you want to have lunch today?"
Causes an immediate anxiety/panic attack because of this illness.
Bulimia and Body Dysmorphic Disorder shall not, and will not
take over me,

I will not let it,

I am stronger than this.

Anonymous, 23 years old

You are
RESILIENT

ANONYMOUS, 18

# *You are resilient*

Hello me, it's you.

It's odd to think at 22 you have graduated from university twice (you didn't even think you would be alive at 15 at one point). Don't feel disheartened that you didn't get the grade you wanted, you were dealing with a lot and I'm proud you battled through it. Right now life is a bit scary with not being sure of what to do, living with anxiety and recovering from an eating disorder which you've had for the past five years. Along the way however I've learnt a lot about myself and the world around me, so I wish to share that with you.

1. Remember when you couldn't get on the school bus because you couldn't breathe, you felt sick and you started hysterically crying? Or when you would wake up in the middle of the night hyperventilating thinking everything in the world was going to go wrong? Or even when you struggled to go outside because you were scared of people looking at you, talking to you or just being around lots of people? Well that was anxiety, you don't find that out 'til you're 20 but it's okay. People are not as scary as you think! No, they don't hate you, one day they will sit down with you and tell you they actually admired you all along for being the person who would dye their hair a different colour every week and make their own clothes. You learn they too suffer with anxiety and understand how you feel. It takes time but you start going to 'Goth nights' and 'Rock nights' at clubs and start talking to people who have the same interests and it gets easier. You make friends, which will help you so much. Don't feel ashamed about struggling to make phone calls or being anxious around new people – you're not being rude, you just need to breathe.

2. Battling through an eating disorder will be the hardest thing you will do so far. You will feel helpless and out of control. I don't want to scare you but at 19 you will have a seizure because of it and end up in hospital. Trust me when I say this, things get better. I know you keep getting told that and you don't believe it; You go from being so severely ill to being so far in recovery,

because you are strong. Yes you relapsed 18 times but you know what? Each time you progress further, you will beat it don't worry. Just keep trying and you will get there. (You will also influence others to choose recovery).

3. When you ask yourself "should I stop drinking?" The answer is yes. Being at university you are surrounded by nights out and drinking but you need to lay off the drink. You will feel embarrassed about drinking too much resulting in countless panic attacks and being sick. Drinking will not solve your problems, it will only worsen them.

4. You will have an amazing academic advisor, lecturer and best friend who all give you great advice and will listen when you need someone. Your advisor is someone who you can talk to, don't be afraid about this. She will help you manage your personal life and academic life. She is also someone who shows you, you are much more capable than you believe. She will give you some of the best life advice – always remember what she says: 'You are resilient' do not forget that. The person who ends up being your best friend is the one you least suspect. You will fight, laugh and cry together but he will make such an impact on your life and vice versa you will not feel alone. (See? As I said earlier, people are not as scary as you think).

5. You'll be selling your artwork at a comic and film convention soon – yes really you will be. Keep practising and it will pay off. Don't feel ashamed to say you have a skill in something, because you do. Art is a great form of escapism and distraction. Do more art, paint everything, and sketch what you see. You will even design some of your tattoos (Right now you hate tattoos but you will change your mind!)

6. And finally keep being you. Don't change yourself to fit in, people like the fact you have different interests. Add all the spikes to the jacket you want, dye your hair odd colours (but put that bleach down! A couple of times are fine but don't overdo it). Want all those nose piercings? Get them, they rock! And be proud of your tattoos (Maxxie the phoenix is our favourite). Society might tell you otherwise but keep being you, because you are awesome.

You will have some hard times ahead worrying about work, friends, family and your own issues – but you always get through it. Just hold on and keep going. Breathe, it will be worth it. You are capable of so much and I am forever proud of you, don't forget that!

The Little Red Cat x

Anonymous, 18 years old

YOU must be
responsible
for your OWN
happiness

ANONYMOUS, 23

# *You must be responsible for your own happiness*

Hello me, it's you.

I know you, like one day you will know me. I know you're reading this and I know you're thinking there's nothing I can possibly say which you don't already know. We know it all, don't we? We listen to advice from others, but we've never used it, because we have a problem. We've always stood alone and we stand by this notion that we know best, because how could anyone possibly know what's best for us, than us? The problem is - we're wrong.

You will never forget those younger years. For most people their childhood is something they fondly remember. Maybe it's something they always try and get back. I know you can't wait to grow up. Ten years old and they made us sit inside at lunch time and watch the other children play. Eleven years old, sitting in that office with the man who we later learned had been a child psychologist. Even today mum and dad have never told me what he said, what he diagnosed. Twelve years old and they packed us off to anger management - therapy for the kids they think will grow up to be serial killers. That was our turning point. Not because sitting in a circle with other "angry children" punching a lump of clay was in any way therapeutic. It was our turning point, because you realised the one thing you wanted more than anything, to "grow up", was slipping away.

You can do anything, I still can. But it was that moment we knew, to do anything we needed to change... and we did. We found books and all those thoughts and feelings we never could control, which would cause us to kick out at the world because it felt like it was always kicking us - we learned to control them. We read and we read, and eventually they went away. That red mist, that rage not forgotten, but gone. And here you are today. You've got into college and it's been half a decade since you've been in trouble and that will continue for a while. I wish I could tell you that it's sunshine from here on out, but it's not. The world is going to kick out again and harder than it ever has, and hopefully ever will.

I'm in Oxford at the moment. Don't get too excited! We didn't get into the "real" Oxford, but we've done pretty well. It's been a hard year so far. You've had a couple of girlfriends. Yes... seriously. I know at this very moment you're planning a solitary life. One dedicated to your books and to nobody but yourself. That will change. I know we're a little slow on the physical maturity side of things (We can almost grow a full beard now), but puberty is going to hit us not like a truck, but more like the way a passenger jet collides with a not--so-self-aware seagull. Don't panic! There's no feathers and fairly little blood involved, but you're going to find our little heart gets itself into quite the state whenever you see girls. Oh, and please note the terrible wordplay here. We've become shamefully fond of that.

Joking aside, you're going to have your heart broken. Not once, but twice. Both times are rough. The second time possibly more so. There's something about betrayal that brings out the very worst in us and it hasn't disappointed thus far. She hurts you. She hurts you so deeply that we start regressing. We become solitary again, but instead of sitting inside at lunch time we succumb to vices you're currently too young to legally partake in. For months I slept all day and drank all night. That anger comes back, full of vengeance and swollen knuckles. Your friends say you're depressed. I think we probably were. Remember seeing those pills by dad's computer desk? They were for depression and even after finding that out I never thought in a thousand life times that I would ever suffer from it. You're a strong person, but it doesn't matter how strong or how independent you are - life can change in a night-time and it's okay. It's okay to hurt. It's okay to be angry. It's okay to be miserable. It's okay because you're not alone. You never have been alone, and even when the night time is long and that sunshine feels like it will always be half the world away - you are not alone.

You start talking to a girl, a friend of a friend and for some reason you feel able to tell her how you're feeling and even then it's okay, because she's felt like this too. She tells you about her counselling and how it's truly helped her and even though I never went, I wish I had. Instead I found a book, a couple of books actually, and once again they save you. You can always count on books. A book will never betray you.

You kicked out. I kicked out. It's very important that I say "I kicked out" because if there's one thing I've learnt through all this is to be responsible. If there's one thing I want you to take away from this is - YOU must be responsible for your own happiness. I'm still healing, but things are once again starting to look brighter. The night time is ending. I wish I could go into more detail, but some things need to be felt rather than read. I have to go now, but remember this always. You're not alone.

Be responsible for your own happiness. Think about what I mean by this, it's not as simple or as selfish as it sounds. Because I think the one thing I've learnt through the course of writing this letter is happiness, true happiness, cannot be found alone. Goodbye me. Don't worry. It's going to be magic.

Anonymous, 23 years old

NEVER look back, walk TALL, act fine

# *Never look back, walk tall, act fine*

Dear sixteen year old me,

As I write this, you would have just finished celebrating what is still to be your best birthday ever; in Liverpool, with the three people you care about most in this world. You go on to make a "Liverpool" wall, with all the wonderful photos you collected over this weekend- you look at it every morning, or when you need cheering up.

First off, I wanted to say you've been through so much this year and still came out smiling in December! You're strong don't forget that, it serves you well in the future. You might not think so right now, having just bid goodbye to your current friendship group. You're probably still pondering over the fact that none of them bothered sharing a celebratory message on your Facebook wall (Note for the future: Facebook is overrated.) You think they must hate you.

Well I'm here to tell you they don't, and they never did. That was all in your imagination I'm afraid. Don't stay inside that head of yours Missy, unless you're daydreaming about boys (you're going to start doing that a whole lot more, believe me!)

Oh, but you know that panic attack you had at the cinema a few months back? There's a lot more of them to come. You're going to end up gripping onto a metal bench, hyperventilating, in an empty train station. I know that sounds bad, but after it's done, you still pluck up the courage to march back into college and finish the school day. But you'll pull through, and have relapses, which gets you upset. You'll leave college and go through a period of having only two people to talk to, wondering if they're even going to stick around (Spoiler Alert: They Do.) You'll feel like a dark cloud is hanging over your head, unsure of when it's going to lift, so here comes the good part:

When you reach nineteen, you realise it's time for change. You start this new treatment called CBT and meet a wonderful woman named Joan (she'll remind you of Gran!). You came off the pill only to realise that had been causing your mood swings this whole time, so you start to feel more stable.

As for the social anxiety, well this is going to blow your mind. Two weeks ago you met up with three lovely women whom you had been conversing with other Twitter to see Let It Be together and you had a brilliant time! You were independent and easy-going; traits you think you're losing now, but they re-surface with a vengeance, let me tell you! And I could not have been more proud.

Finally, you're just about to come across a certain musical legend, so I'll leave you with what is currently one of your favourite lyrics of his: Never look back, walk tall, act fine.

Love the Nineteen Year Old You.

Anonymous, 19 years old

You are
your own
NUMBER
ONE

# *You are your own number one*

Hello me, it's you

I'll try and keep this short but there are a few points I want to attend to.

Number one is; you are your own number one.
You tried for so long but it was time to move on.
I know you crave this feeling to belong.
I know you crave this feeling that you mean something to someone.
But don't you see that someone was always you.
You are worthy of your own time now you'll never be number two.

Number two; nobody really knows how lonely you are.
When you sit in a full room and still feel alone.
I don't know if this feeling will ever go but believe me when I say
you are not on your own.
It's scary but true
That wall you built around yourself someone broke through.
So don't push her away, I know it's so easy to do.


Number three; you're afraid of people knowing the real you
because you don't believe you're nice.
Your moods are dangerous
Your heart is made of ice.
You know your inner evil and it scares you to your core.
Sometimes when your venom hits
You can't stop the blood pour.
But hurt is real. You did not inflict the pain.
You got to learn to forgive yourself or you will drive yourself
insane.
You can't hold onto grudges or we will never get through the
weather.
People do love you, everything will get better.


Number four; I know you want a quick fix but it's not going to
happen.
The world invites self-hate. We will break the habit.
I know you can't take a compliment and you can't take critique.

You are at constant war with yourself.
You perceive yourself as weak.
I promise you, you view yourself wrong
I know you can't see it now but you are unbelievably strong.

Number five; I know you feel empty. I know you feel unsure
Nobody knows, nobody knows no more than yourself.
We are all in the same water just on a different boat.
And I know it's so easy to compare yourself
to the ones that sink
to the ones that float
But no one really has it smooth sailing. It's easy option to quit
when you're too afraid of failing.
You are not drowning, you are more than capable.
So please tell yourself everyday
You are inspirational.
So when you think you can't do things, tell yourself you can.

Love sincerely
Your biggest fan

Anonymous, 21 years old

GRIT your TEETH & focus on _YOU_

# *Grit your teeth and focus on you*

Hello me, it you

Firstly, I've got to give you a high five for being as strong as you have been so far and then you're going to need a big hug because unfortunately it's got to get harder before it gets better. You've just turned 16 and this year is probably going to be the most defining of your life so far, in fact, 6 years on, you're still going to be giving it a great deal of thought. You will have your first serious love interest and also have your heart broken so just remember to keep your friends close, I promise you they will never leave you. We did it, we got to university, and we get to make art and study history every day, so you see, its already a lot better than you ever thought it could be.

You won't believe me now, but trust me, you and mum will eventually be able to forgive each other for how the last 10 years have been between you two. You'll learn to understand the way she is, how she has a problem with drink and that it wasn't you that was the cause to all the violence and pain she inflicted on you. It wasn't ever your fault, though I'm not sure how long it's going to take us to forgive her, but she has her own problems, ones we can't fix or help, so concentrate on doing the best for yourself because I promise the emotional abuse will fade soon and you'll see a light that you never thought would appear.

Dad is going to leave. It won't be a surprise really, but it will surprise you how much your heart is broken when he does. Please try not to ignore that pain. Numbing it with alcohol will not help you, and neither mum or your sister is going to be in a state to notice you are hurting, so please don't be hurting yourself as a cry for help, just cry, let it out. Help will find you. When the teachers at school ask you if you want to speak to a counsellor, turn up to that appointment, don't freak out on the day, because the problems in your mind now will only follow you for years. You're so strong, you just don't know it yet.

School is so important. You may not think it now, in fact you are plotting ways to miss days at a time already, whether that be to stay on the train longer than your stop, or to hide until mum has left for work, but please, your friends are the most stable element in your life, don't waste time by not seeing them.

In sixth form you are going to be trusted with your own freedom in terms of attending school, don't abuse this. Unfortunately as you know, mum won't take any interest in your school life, and no matter how many meetings she has to have with the head teacher, she won't notice enough to make you attend, so stop trying to make her see you, she needs to work that one out on her own. Get yourself to school and people will stop calling you lazy and maybe see you are hurting. If you give people reason to think that you just can't be bothered, then how are they going to see you need a helping hand. You can do it.

Don't you dare let go of your best friends. They love you to pieces and you need them so much. Family may be blood, but your friendship with those girls is going to get you through a hell of a lot. When you feel the need to hurt yourself, just think about how much they love you and how much you'd hurt them if you took yourself away from their lives. When it gets to that time of night when the only thing you know how to control is your own pain, don't inflict more on yourself, just talk to one of them, they will never ever judge you. Those scars you make now are going to haunt you for the next 6 years as people ask where they were from. You can lie, you always do, but wouldn't it be easier to never have them in the first place? Get that help you have been craving. Go to the doctors, it will only take one trip and all the pain will begin to fade away.

Your best friends are all going to go to uni soon and you're going to be the only one left at home on a gap year, so get out there, do something with your free time! I know it's hard, I know you freeze at the thought of talking to strangers, but break through now and you will be more prepared when you start uni in September. Anxiety will never go away, but learn to accept that people want to get to know you, not everyone is out to hurt or embarrass you, and you have a voice, use it!

So for now, I'm just going to leave you with this. Know that you and your sister and going to finally become friends and that mum will calm down eventually. For now, grit your teeth and focus on you. Love your friends like they deserve, you will love them even more in 6 years, they will get you through.

Stay strong, learn to cry, learn to love and finally learn to accept yourself because when you do you will open up your heart to everyone who has been trying to get in when you didn't want to know. And hey, you may have thought you'd missed your chance by the end of third year, but you will find that someone you have been looking for, in the most unexpected place, and it will feel like it was meant to be all along.

Anonymous, 22 years old

you are
my
hero

ANONYMOUS, 22

# *You are my hero*

Hello me,

It must be around this time, 8 years ago in 2007. You've probably started to notice Dad is getting worse. You've probably noticed he's very sharp, judgemental and is saying mean things to both you and Mum. He shouts and shouts and gets very angry and upset over the little things that don't matter.

You feel like every move you've made is the wrong move, because he tells you so. You've spoken incorrectly, you're fidgeting, you wear too much makeup, you need to listen, you need to stop talking, you don't need her as a friend, you need her as a friend.

I've heard these words before and so have you.

"You are stupid."
"You don't ever listen to me, because you don't care."
"I know what's right for you."
"Grow up."
"Get out of my sight."

I know it feels like you want to cry, I know it's made you cry.

"Why are you crying?"
"Stop crying, for goodness sake, stop crying!"
"Get over it!"

I know you stop and think daily why you aren't good enough for him, why you can't get anything right, why you can't get along or love him the way you imagined and when this stressful stage of life will stop so you can be free of it all. So you can be you, really be you. Because I know, all of this, somehow made you feel different. Made you feel like you didn't really belong or you'll never be able to truly be yourself. You can't quite grasp why and trust me; I'm still trying to figure it out. But you are strong and I am forever grateful at how strong you are, because you've made me a better person. However the fact remains. He's not well. He's sick and I'm sorry, it's going to get worse. He's going to scream at you and Mum on Christmas Eve, about being a little bit late leaving for a party. The thing is you're outside ready to get into the car and that's when it escalates, he starts shouting, people walking by are watching. You're going to feel embarrassed, sad and angry. You will cry. Because he tells you both to fuck off, tells you that he won't be there in the morning and that you can spend Christmas without him. You cry because you don't want that, you don't want any of this. You run back inside and you spend Christmas Eve in your room and fall asleep with a pillow full of tears with Mum by your side, feeling like the world had ended and that you'll never see your Dad again.

You wake up the next day and he is there waiting for you. With open arms, like nothing happened. You feel like screaming in his face "WHAT'S WRONG WITH YOU?" But you don't, because your natural instinct will tell you not you, because you are strong. Several weeks later you'll go to an appointment with Dad with a Doctor you've not seen before. Between that time from Christmas Eve to the appointment, your Mum was brave enough and strong enough to face your Dad and tell him he's not well and that he needs help. It was a struggle but she managed to convince him to face his problem, which he knew deep inside, he had to. The Doctor will ask you questions and want you to be completely honest. Although you feel terrified in doing so, wondering what Dad might say after it all, whether he will shout at you again, you do it anyway and it will break your Dad's heart but it will mend it much faster because of your words. The Doctor will ask, "When was last time he showed a sign of extreme anger or upset?"

You tell the Doctor, who listens to you, about Christmas Eve. You tell Dad how it made you feel and he will cry. He will break down and tell you he's sorry and thank you for being so honest. The Doctor explains to you, your Dad has a case of depression and that the reason behind his behaviour for so long is because of this. This time will make you reflect on years of your life beforehand and how the signs were obvious even back then. You pity Dad, for how he must have felt inside all these years. But you can't help but feel like your relationship with him will never be the same. He has hurt your feelings one too many times.

Years go by and he improves and he doesn't have to take the medication anymore, but you will never truly believe it really cured him. Because there are some moments in which you won't want to remember, but you will have to go through them and be strong. Just be strong. Your Mum will need you to be strong for her also. Because she loses a sister, your Auntie L and her guard is down for some time. I'm sorry. But remember you are strong.

Even now, there are times I wonder if Dad is sick again. But you and Dad do eventually have a better relationship. We found ground with each other. I stand up to him (believe it or not.) I spend more time with him. Some times are difficult, but I cope because you were strong. I'm beginning to notice however, how much I am like him. From my manners, the way I speak, the way I think. My eyes are his. I like the things he likes. But… I get upset over the little things, but just as much as the big. I get angry a lot, but never release it.

I stormed out in an argument with both Mum and Dad, saying I'd not be coming back.

I don't feel happy right now E and I'm scared. I'm scared I'm going to be like Dad, I'm scared I am not as strong as you anymore and weakness is creeping into me slowly and I can't stop it. But, my life is not miserable; you have so much to look forward to. I am surrounded by many things to be happy about; close friends, new family, following the dream, education, kittens, a lover who typically breaks my heart but is one of my close friends in time, opportunities and better health. Just whatever you do, be strong. In the meantime, I will be working on myself.

You are my hero, forever and always.

Love,
You.

Anonymous, 22 years old

I Can't WAIT
to see
what you do
next

# *I can't wait to see what you do next*

Hello me, it's you.

You don't know it yet but you've got anxiety. You'll find out soon enough, in about a year or so, and from that point on I promise you things will get so much better. I'm 19 now (nearly 20 which is utterly terrifying! How are we so old?!) and over the past few years you've come a long way.

First off I'm going to say what hundreds of people have told you thousands of times: don't worry. This may not seem like the most original or insightful advice from your future self but I'm telling you not to worry because I know that you're going to be ok. Remember when you thought you wouldn't get through that history lesson where you had to stand up and give a presentation? Well you did and three years on you're still going and you're doing great! Right now everything seems scary and you feel crap. You've isolated yourself from your friends and as far as your family know you're 'fine'. But you're really not and it's ok to not be fine. Lots of people experience mental illness and you're one of them. It's not your fault that you're experiencing anxiety but it's up to you to take the first step to get help. That means talking to someone, which is scary, and having to talk to someone about this is even scarier but it's what you need to do.

Things get harder before they get easier. You'll drive yourself to your first counselling appointment (yep you can drive!) with expectations that are through the roof and you'll leave feeling disappointed and tearful. It's not the miracle cure or a quick-fix you'll hope for, but the more you go the more it helps so don't give up! One day you're going to look back on all this as a distant memory and hopefully you'll feel proud of yourself because it's hard and it's horrible but you're going to get through it.

Right now you're worrying about GCSEs so you're throwing yourself into work. I know that you're convinced that anything less than straight A*s is failure and that you're comparing yourself to your brother. I hate to break it to you but you don't get straight A*s, not even straight As, as on results day you open that envelope and there's a B smiling up at you. That's all you see and you're oblivious to anything else. But you know what? You actually did really well and that B in physics doesn't matter; besides you know that you're not a sciencey person. By now you'll have realised your deep love of history and you use the past as an escape. It's true that in many ways you've got it better than people centuries ago who were being executed left, right and centre and being ravaged by plague but that doesn't mean you can dismiss your problems!

History is still a big part of your life as you'll study it at uni where you're going to have an amazing time! You're going to live in the centre of a gorgeous city, make friends, read stacks of books, decide that you like gin and develop greater appreciation of your parents. In the beginning being surrounded by new people is terrifying and exhausting but it's also the best environment for you to push yourself in. Sure, it's a slow process but it's getting better and that's what counts! You've got the most incredible group of friends who you have the silliest/weirdest conversations with, who make you laugh and are always ready to own the dancefloor with you. You've had some of your best moments with them and some of your worst. The whole perfectionist thing isn't quite sorted but we're getting there. Last term got quite bad, but evenings crumpled on the bathroom floor crying and hyperventilating helped you realise that you've still got a way to go and this time round you were more prepared to get help.

You've come so far in the past three years and can keep going. There's bound to be a few bumps in the road but you've overcome them before and can do it again. Just keep looking after yourself and living your life. I can't wait to see what you do next. x

Anonymous, 19 years old

I looked
for HELP.
I found it.

# *I looked for help. I found it.*

Suicidal thoughts.

I was thinking about them. Suicidal thoughts. Mine used to be common and they would vary in severity. Alone, crying every drop of my soul out to just quietly getting through my day, Surrounded.

Apathetic. Should I make a cup of tea or kill myself? Finish this essay or kill myself? Go for a walk or kill myself? Reply to this text or kill myself? Should I kill myself?

I used to think my suicidal thoughts were just something I'd have forever, like the mole above lip or the persistent (little bastard) hair on my left nipple. Killing myself was always an option. A comforting thought. A familiarity.

I guess deep down I didn't really want to do it. Not really. I never even self harmed. "Illegitimate" depression? Unworthy? Hypochondriac? Just get on with it. Attention seeker.

Would I overdose? Jump? Hang? I never went into it much. I wanted to die, I didn't want to do it. Instead, I'd fantasise about my death. Soothing. Comforting.

If I was to die I'd like it to be an accident. I'd think. A bus crash, where only I die - a daydream of mine. I particularly liked to day dream about dying while on the bus. Daze.

12 to 21.
I was sad. Always sad. Terribly miserable. On and off.

Now.
I hardly ever think about killing myself. I hardly ever imagine my death. I'm not always happy. Sometimes I am happy. But I'm not depressed.

Hindsight.
I didn't even realise I was - was depressed, that is. I thought everyone must have suicidal thoughts. Of course everyone

routinely thinks about killing themselves. Of course everyone fights with their own head daily. You're not special.

It shouldn't be routine to think about killing yourself. Mundane, lonely routine. Maybe once in a while. It's ok to be not ok.

21.
I looked for help. I found it. You shouldn't want to die.

Now.
I'm not always happy, but I'm not depressed.

Anonymous, 23 years old

# IT'S OKAY to watch others SUCCEED

ANONYMOUS, 21

# It's okay to watch others succeed

There is no one alive who is you-er than you.

I firstly want you to know how hard it is for me to sit down
and write this letter. It took me forever to realise that this is
an exercise that will only help my current self heal because I
know how much you need to heal, therefore I'm doing this
for you. I know how much you are hurting. I know how
much you are screaming for someone to listen. But I need
you to know one thing, the only person who truly needs
to listen – is yourself. You are doing the best you can. With
the circumstances around you, you are trying hard enough;
and God, I know how much you don't think it, but you are
succeeding. Knowing the things that I know now, and having

come to terms with everything I know now, I now have learnt to understand you so much more.

There is no one alive who is you-er than you.
You are just a kid dealing with something not even a grandparent could deal with. Your thoughts, feelings, emotions, particularly your anger, is justifiable. You have been handed a circumstance that you don't deserve, but the biggest and greatest solution to the overall problem is realising that you actually, in fact, do deserve this. You are special, unique and so amazing, that the only person who doesn't think that is you.
There is no one alive who is you-er than you.

All the doubts, fears, and made up scenarios in your head are materialistic and tangible. They go away. You stay. You live. You make it through. Even for me now this is incredibly hard to write because I wish my 30 year old self could talk to me now and tell me that I do make it through. Because the only thing you live on is hope. Yes, hope works, but hope isn't as strong and as powerful as the faith you have within yourself – the faith IN YOURSELF.

There is no one alive who is you-er than you.
The world constantly tries and tries to put you down. And the problem is that because of how many times it tries, you've

started to believe it. The only person who can ever get you down is you. You have the mindful power to create any situation you want to create for yourself. Nobody can get to you if only you believe in yourself and your abilities.

There is no one alive who is you-er than you.
Love. It is your greatest and most powerful gift for the world. You are so great at it, and everyone is so drawn to you because of it. Believe in yourself. Believe that you have the courage, the will to persevere. Learn that even if someone gets you down, that learning to love them for it is the best form of forgiveness. Forgiving others isn't for their benefit, but for your own peace. Trust. Trust those that you love. Trust those that give you life. Because they settle very specifically into your heart.

There is no one alive who is you-er than you.
Remember that it's ok to watch others succeed. It's ok to be second best. It's ok to fail. It's ok to be down. Because it's those moments that allow you to learn and to grow and to develop this amazing character that you are.

There is no one alive who is you-er than you.
And the greatest thing you need to know, is to not judge. I don't mean physical appearance; but more situations. People have their own life to live. Their own concerns, their own battles, their own stories. Because they hurt you, doesn't mean

that it is a reflection of who you are, but more because it is a reflection of what they are dealing with. What they needed to do for them. And just because that hurt you, does not mean it has any reflection on who you are.

And no matter how hard and tough life gets, you can make it through, because there is no one alive who is you-er than you.

Anonymous, 21 years old

- your -
# FEELINGS
## matter

ANONYMOUS, 21

## *Your feelings matter*

Dear 16 year old me.

First of all, it's real. The feelings you feel are real. They are yours and they affect you and they are real. In fact it all affects you. I know you think you are coping fine and it doesn't affect you and that you're not bothered. But you are. You are bothered. You are completely bothered. But you continue to bottle it up. (If I'm being honest with you, I still bottle it up but I'm learning. We'll get there).

You put so much pressure on yourself that it's no wonder that you have outbursts. You're angry. You're afraid. You're unbelievably sad. And you can't understand these emotions.

Yet you still laugh, you joke, you sing and dance and you're silly –beyond silly. You're spontaneous and you know how to have fun. People actually tell you how much they love your company so how come you're the only one who can't? I ask this because I'm speaking to myself now. I just hope 5 years down the line our 26 year old self is telling us how much she loves herself.

I have hope.

And I know you are full of hope too and I sometimes think that's the problem. You hope too much that you fall hard. You rate people too high that they let you down. You get too excited about the fantasy of it all that reality makes you depressed. In fact writing this letter has made me realise that we possibly have bipolar disorder. (I promise we will go the doctors about this). What you are suffering with now is depression; but don't worry you will go, avoid and go again to a counsellor. We went to a few before finding the right one. She makes you understand things about yourself and how you say 'I don't know' when you do. It just feels uncomfortable saying how you feel out loud. She helps you realise how much you can't take a compliment and how uncomfortable that makes you feel as well. She also gives you tips on how to take them (receive them like you would a birthday present …accept it, say thank you and think about how nice it was for them to do/say that). She also points out how you run away from everything. You know it's true. You sabotage relationships so you can be unhappy on your own terms. I guess it's because you're afraid of people not being there for you so you don't give them the chance.

At the moment you are thinking no one understands you and that you don't belong. You have already fantasised about death but never to actually harm or kill yourself. You just get comfort of the idea of not existing or for your head to explode because too much is going on in there. It's because you overthink and overanalyse and never express them in a healthy way. You continue to lash out and try so hard to push more and more people out your life. But you know the best people stayed. You have people in your life that love you; regardless of the amount of times you tried to push them away. But be careful, they are human too. Don't allow your self-destruction destroy the people you love.

Although, I'm supposed to be writing this from the other side I don't think I'm quite there yet. But here are my tips to you (and to remind myself);

Happiness isn't a destination and it isn't even a journey. It is an emotion and emotions can be fleeting. You have just got to recognise and cherish those moments when they happen.

And soon you'll realise how many moments in a day you feel happy. So when you're down take that hour long bus ride to nowhere and back, go on long walks, speak or smile to a stranger, help someone in need, laugh out loud, give a genuine compliment, play basketball in the park, play on the swings like you're flying in the sky, sing while you're walking down the street, fall in love and let someone fall in love with you, give people 20+ second long hugs, ask for help when you need it, cry when you need to, cry for nothing, stand up for something and don't let anyone take away you're childish soul. You don't have to have extraordinary days to have a good day. Find the happiness in the mundane. And you will realise that you are happy in the same way that you are sad and angry. They are meant to be felt not lived, remember to not let these emotions consume you.

I just want you to know that your feelings matter.

Anonymous, 21 years old

IT'S _OKAY_
not to feel
_OKAY_
SOMETIMES

# *It's okay not to feel okay sometimes*

Hello me, it's you, five years on.

Yes, you've made it to 21! You don't know it just yet, but you're about to move to the other side of the country, leaving your school, friends, house and everything familiar to you. Except for your, currently undiagnosed, depression and anxiety.

I won't pretend that the next few months aren't going to be incredibly difficult for you to cope with, you are going to feel very scared and very alone for a long time. You will first seek help through the counselling service at your new college, a pleasant and kind lady's advice and guidance will help a considerable amount towards you finally settling into your new college, home and life.

But your worries, anxieties and suicidal thoughts aren't situational I'm afraid, they're a mental health illness and it's still going to take you a few years before you start to understand this better. Your boyfriend won't help, I'm not even sure he knows to this day just how much you were silently suffering at the time, but it will teach you some incredibly valuable lessons about love, relationships and how much you will value your close friends and your relationship with your sometimes difficult, but always loving, family.

You will see seven different councillors, therapists, doctors and alternative remedy doctors by the time you are 21. Each one will have an impact on your life and help you in some way, but without wanting to scare you I regret to say you will have to deal with most of this on your own. Health anxiety is a very confusing and frustrating thing for you, and others, to understand but that said, I am incredibly proud of our progress, 16 year old me, you are doing so well.

Always remember that you are not defined by your mental health issues. It's exhausting and isolating dealing with both the mental and physical sides of anxiety and depression, but you will make some amazing friends that make this so much easier for you to deal with and understand. You will learn how to deal with your panic attacks, depressive episodes and health anxieties, sometimes it will be a case of waiting it out and that's okay, you're allowed to not feel okay sometimes.

Buckle up, 16 year old me, it's going to be a rollercoaster but the ups are definitely worth the downs, I promise.

Anonymous, 21 years old

# WHERE TO GO NEXT?

*It is important to seek help if you've been affected by anything in this book.*

If you need immediate medical help, feel like hurting yourself or others, please go to **A&E for emergency support** or call your local emergency services (UK: 999).

**Make an appointment with your GP**, they are trained to deal with mental health problems as well as physical ailments and can point you in the direction of your local counselling service. The waiting list for counselling services can be lengthy depending on your location, ask how long the waiting times are so you're fully informed. It's worth considering if you're able to afford private counselling as well. Discuss this with your GP. Though this can be hard, and sometimes induces anxiety itself, it's important to persevere. Perhaps ask if a friend or family member can come with you, or let the doctor know that you find this difficult.

Listening services such as **The Samaritans** are on-hand 24 hours a day, 365 days a year. This service is ideal if you need someone to talk to immediately about how you are feeling. Whilst a fantastic service to those who are suicidal, you don't have to be suicidal to call. They are applicable for anyone who needs someone to listen.

The number for the Samaritans is: 116 123 (UK) and is free to call from any mobile or landline.

You can also email the Samaritans at: jo@samaritans.org which can be really helpful for those who have difficulty verbalising feelings or using phones.

**Reaching out to friends and family** or other loved ones can feel like a huge step. If you're experiencing mental health issues, or feel like you need to talk to a loved one, this can be the first step to getting help. One in four people have mental health issues, and you may be surprised at your shared experiences or their wish to offer support.

**If someone reaches out to you for help** with mental health issues, remember they are not expecting you to 'fix' them. Offering to listen and to help find further resources or even accompanying them to GP appointments could make all the difference.

*Writing things down can help, turn to the next page to have a go at writing a letter to your younger self...*

For more information and further resources visit;
www.hellomeitsyou.org

**TRY WRITING A LETTER TO YOUR YOUNGER SELF...**

*No rules, no right, no wrong;*

*just your story.*

hello me, it's you...

_____

_____

_____

_____

_____

_____

_____

_____

_____

_____

_____

_____

_____

_____

_____

_____

_____

_____

_____
_____
_____
_____
_____
_____
_____
_____
_____
_____
_____
_____
_____
_____
_____
_____
_____
_____
_____
_____
_____
_____
_____

If you would like to submit your letter for the opportunity to feature in the next edition of Hello Me, It's You then head over to our website at www.hellomeitsyou.org and go to the submissions page, where you can find help and guidlines on how to do so!

HAN & JEN

## *Thank You*

And that's the end of our book. We really really do hope it has helped you or will help you or those around you in the future. We hope you've taken away a positive message and perhaps realised you're not alone. But most of all we hope you have hope too.

Hannah          Jenny

# CONNECT WITH US

www.hellomeitsyou.org

 HELLO ME, IT'S YOU

 hellomeitsyou@gmail.com

 @ HELLOMEITSYOU

 # HELLOMEITSYOU

 HELLO ME, IT'S YOU

I looked for HELP. I found it. on YOU IT'S OKAY to watch others SUCCEED You are your own NUMBER ONE BELIE you m he

I can't WAIT to see what you do NEXT you CAN get through this I can't WAIT to see what you do NEVER look back, walk TALL, act fine you

GRIT your TEETH & focus on YOU you are STRONG Be the person you've always wanted to be in a mirror you are MORE than a REFLECTION OF YOU You are RESILIENT never FORGET to TAKE CARE OF YOU keep being DON'T the w CHANG

never FORGET to TAKE CARE OF YOU NEVER look back, walk TALL, act fine that Talking about it all IS OKAY, not wanting to IS OKAY too GRIT your TEETH & focus on YOU I looked for HELP. I found it. not you, I can't WAIT to see what you do NEXT

you are my hero You are your own NUMBER ONE YOU must be responsible for your OWN happiness you CAN get through this

keep Smiling & being you. DON'T let the world CHANGE YOU you are STRONG you are MORE than a You are RESILIENT you are excellent & you will contin to be so, so DO GIVE UP, maybe a cry and then WRITE IT all down TRUST ME Crack on stay

You are your own NUMBER ONE

you are my hero

YOU must be responsible for your OWN happiness

you CAN get through this

BELIEVE in it.

but YOURSELF

NEVER look back. walk TALL, act fine

you are STRONG

I can't WAIT to see what you do NEXT

Stay TRUE STAY

stay hap

You are RESILIENT

keep Smiling

being you. DON'T let the world CHANGE YOU

you are excellent you will continue to be so, so DON'T GIVE UP, maybe have a cry and then Crack on.

are never FORGET to TAKE CARE OF YOU

WE'RE making it there is LIGHT

I would like you to know that THERE IS SOMEBODY out there who loves you

GRIT your TEETH focus on YOU

I looked for HELP. I found it.

NOBODY can change how YOU feel inside but YOURSELF

No MATTER what love throws at you, you have to BELIEVE in it.

YOU must be responsible for your OWN happiness

you CAN get through this

NEVER look back. walk TALL, act fine

you are my hero

You are RESILIENT

you are excellent you will continue to be so, so DON'T GIVE UP, maybe have a cry and then Crack on.

WRITE IT all down

you are STRONG

TRUST ME

stay TRUE

GRIT your